# Finance &
# BUDGETING FOR
# LINE MANAGERS

*Anthony Greenall*

*The Industrial Society*

First published in 1996 by
The Industrial Society
Robert Hyde House
48 Bryanston Square
London W1H 7LN
Telephone: 0171 479 2000

© *The Industrial Society 1993*
*Reprinted 1998, 1999*
ISBN 1 85835 431 5
ref: 569 PUB 2.99
**British Library Cataloguing-in-Publication Data.**
**A cataloguing record for this book is available from the**
**British Library.**

Typeset by:GCS
Printed by: Optichrome Limited
Cover design: Rhodes Design

The Industrial Society is a Registered Charity No. 290003

# Contents

# Acknowledgements

I would like to thank first of all my colleagues in our publications department for their patience and help with the various drafts of this book.

Particular thanks are also due to Carol McKeown for typing the drafts for me.

Additionally, I would like to thank Andrew Cameron, our Finance Director, for his suggestions on reading the text; any problems that remain, however, are all mine.

Anthony Greenall
May 1996

# Introduction:   A guide to the structure of the book

This is a book of two topics (financial awareness and budgeting) which, whilst they could be read separately (as parts 1 and 3 respectively), are nonetheless connected (by part 2).

The first part deals with background financial awareness. It is our experience at The Industrial Society in training line managers in budgeting, that it is often the background knowledge of finance that people need most, in order to "place" what they have to do in preparing and using departmental budgets.

The last part (three) of the book deals with the budgeting process: the success of which, in truth, may depend as much, if not more, on an organised approach as on financial skills or technical knowledge. However, in looking at capital budgets, the opportunity has been taken to look at capital investment appraisal techniques.

Elsewhere in the book the second section including financial ratios may serve to link some issues resulting from overall financial assessment of the business, to policy requirements placed on those involved in budget preparation.

Finance, like any professional discipline, has a jargon all of its own and this in itself can be a barrier to understanding. Whilst an attempt has been made to explain terms used within the text of the book, there is also, as an appendix, a glossary of terms. This may help, but it is only fair to say that it is very difficult to give universal coverage of all terms: not least because most organisations tend to develop their own procedures and terminology as well. If this book enables the reader to get to grips with that, by putting him or her in a position to talk to the financial specialists more easily, it will have served its purpose.

# Part One: Background to financial awareness

Understanding financial accounts is something most of us feel we should master but frequently shy away from because either the jargon, the concepts or the mechanics they employ seem baffling.

Breaking through these barriers is not as difficult as it seems. In the following pages we will:

a) Explain a few, simple concepts which hold the key to the way the year-end accounts of a business are structured.

b) Look at "what goes where" (and why) in the Balance Sheet and Profit & Loss Account (or Income and Expenditure Account for non profit-making organisations).

c) In the context of the above, identify the meaning of various bits of accounting jargon (see also Appendix 1 "A Glossary of Terms").

# 1 Some basic concepts

1 Cash surplus and profit are not the same thing.
2 Both cash flow and profit therefore have to be accounted for and controlled.
3 The Profit & Loss Account is about the viability of the business in terms of its operation or trading (the purpose for which it exists).

   Non-profit making organizations have an Income & Expenditure Account instead, which reveals either a surplus or deficit (see also Glossary of Terms in Appendix 1).
4 Cash flow or liquidity is about ensuring that money is not tied up in such a way that it cannot be used when needed.
5 The Balance Sheet is about the form in which the wealth or assets of the business are held and where the finance for this has come from.

Let us see what these ideas mean, starting with some easy illustrations.

Mr Micawber (in Charles Dickens' "David Copperfield") said:

*"Annual income twenty pounds, annual expenditure nineteen pounds nineteen shillings and sixpence, result happiness. Annual income twenty pounds, annual expenditure twenty pounds ought and sixpence, result misery."*

Today, although we should still be very careful about the circumstances in which we go into debt, allowing our cash outflow to (temporarily) exceed our income may not always be the road to ruin, provided our longer-term viability (or, if you like, our "personal profitability") is sound.

For instance, I may show on my end year bank-balance that I am overdrawn (cash flow situation), but if I know that it is because I deliberately ran up an overdraft, with the bank's agreement, to purchase a new car during the year it could be a perfectly manageable situation. Knowing that this entails a level of expenditure which I will only incur perhaps once every 4 or 5 years, I can look at this expenditure as being spread over the 4 or 5 year period from which I will derive the benefit of having the car – and on that basis conclude that I am not living beyond my means: that I am still "viable" from the standpoint of Profit & Loss Account principles.

Organisations do just this when they purchase fixed assets which they need for running the business (such as premises, equipment etc.) and spread out the cost over a number of years (rather than as a lump sum) when charging it to the Profit & Loss Account – by means of depreciation.

Again, suppose I start a small business making wooden furniture and purchase a wood-turning lathe for £20,000. If I were to charge the whole cost of that against the first year's trading income (which might be quite small) the business may show a loss. Apparently indicating lack of viability, I might conclude from the loss that I should close the business. Common sense, however, says that I have in fact purchased an asset which will give me the wherewithal to make furniture for a number of years to come, and so it seems reasonable to spread the cost over the whole period for which the cost has been incurred and the business will derive benefit. If I therefore estimate that the lathe will last for 5 years, then I can charge £4,000 p.a. depreciation to the Profit & Loss Account rather than the whole £20,000 in one go.

Clearly, employing the concept of depreciation is one reason why the cash flow and profit positions of a business will diverge. The capital expenditure on the fixed asset (£20,000 in the above example) is an immediate cash outflow, whereas the impact on profit is only partially felt in the first year via depreciation and continues at that level (£4,000 p.a.) for a number of years thereafter.

What really happens at the point of acquiring the asset is that the business elects to hold its assets in a different form: £20,000 less in cash, £20,000 more in fixed assets. Depreciation represents that proportion of the value of the asset that the business has used up for the period or year, once the asset is put to use. This switch in asset values will be reflected in the Balance Sheet, which tables how the wealth of the organisation is held.

Much the same happens with stocks or materials. We only

charge material costs to the profit and Loss Account as they are used or converted into sales – stocks of unused, partly-processed materials or finished stocks are assets (to be used in the next year's trading). For example, if a market trader purchases fruit wholesale at the outset he or she is only switching assets from cash to stock. If at the end of a day's selling, the trader wishes to check the profit made it would be on the basis of sales less the cost of the fruit sold. Unsold fruit remaining in stock is still an asset (and if sold the following day will represent part of that next day's costs in due course). However, any stock in an unsaleable condition would have to be written off as a charge against profit.

The Profit and Loss (P&L) Account as a measure of viability also embraces another major difference in the treatment of expenditure (and also sales) relative to cash flow. In the P&L we are concerned with value and matching costs to the level of business done, regardless of when the cash flow takes place.

The reason for this is that if we were not to include some of our invoiced costs in the P&L simply because we had not paid the bill, then clearly we could delude ourselves with an over-statement of profit.

Similarly, if an invoice has not been received for benefits received then we have to "accrue" for it by making an estimate of the amount and charging this figure instead. Any under or over estimate will have to be adjusted in the next period, but at least the difference should be fairly minor compared with ignoring the charge altogether.

In the same way, provided sales have been achieved and evidenced (e.g. goods despatched against an order and invoiced) then they can be counted as income for the P&L

even if payment has not been received. However, if it is clear that payment will not be received, the amount would have to be written off instead as a bad debt and a reduction in profit.

Provisions for (possible but not definite) bad debts are described in the Glossary in Appendix 1.

It is not enough for a business to be able to show that it is viable by recording profits. Indeed, it is not failure to record profits so much as failure to control liquidity (cash-flow) that is the greater immediate cause of a business going "bust".

For instance, if an enterprise is slow in collecting its debts in terms of getting cash from customers it may not have enough cash to continue to pay for its continuing costs (wages and salaries, purchases, overheads etc.) This situation can be exacerbated when a business is expanding, as costs have to be incurred and paid for at an expanding rate ahead of the increase in sales income being received. Trying to expand too rapidly is known as over-trading.

In considering cash-flow, not only are we concerned with the amount of cash or overdraft and how quickly customers (our debtors) pay their bills, but also what payments the business is due to make to suppliers (our creditors). It can also be useful to look at stocks which can be converted into sales and eventually cash. Putting all these elements together we can define what is commonly referred to as "working capital" although it usually appears on the Balance Sheet as "Net Current Assets".

This is how the calculation is made:

| | | |
|---|---|---|
| Stock + Debtors + Cash | = | Current Assets |
| Creditors payable within 12 months* | = | Current Liabilities |
| Current Assets – Current Liabilities | = | Working Capital |

(*Anything already due for payment in less than 12 months is regarded as a current liability. Any liability already incurred for settlement in more than 12 months is a long term liability and probably has more to do with the funding structure of the business – such as a "debenture" loan as an alternative to raising more capital from new share issues. Working capital as the name implies is more concerned with the cash flows in running the business on a day-to-day basis.)

We are obviously keen to see that the working capital calculation results in a positive balance i.e. the cash and near cash (debtors, stocks) is enough to cover the cash outflows due to creditors.

In managing the cash-flow it is important to ensure that cash movements are forecasted or budgeted for control purposes e.g. ensuring that we do not plough money into capital investment in fixed assets without regard to what the working capital needs of the business will be; not allowing customers to hang on to our money without pressing them for payment; controlling the rate at which we release payments to our own suppliers etc.

In addition to being able to find the working capital or "Net Current Assets" figure on the Balance Sheet, we can also see the value of Fixed Assets, calculated on the basis of cost less depreciation to date i.e. their remaining value for future use.

If we add the Fixed Assets and Net Current Assets totals together we have the book value of the business before deducting any long term liabilities. This does not relate to the market value of the business any more than the cost of building a house determines what someone else may be prepared to pay for it.

On the Balance Sheet, the wealth of the business after deducting the long-term liabilities is equal to the total of the sources from which it has been funded: capital from the issue of shares and "Reserves" that have been ploughed back into the business e.g. the cumulative total over the years of retained profit from the P&L Account (retained profit being the remaining balance of profit after deduction of corporation tax and dividend).

Reserves are therefore important in funding growth. Having been absorbed into funding the asset structure of the business, reserves therefore do not exist as a cash amount. Reserves indicate how funding has been increased & the asset structure shows how capital & reserves have been invested.

We are now at a level of detail where it will be helpful to see how this is laid out in terms of "what goes where" in the final (year end) accounts of a business in Chapter 2 of this handbook.

## 2 "What goes where" in the published accounts of a business

### XYZ plc

"as at" – the last day of the financial year. The balance sheet is a " stock take" of assets liabilities as they stand on that particular date

**Balance sheet as at ...**

| | £000's | What the items mean |
|---|---|---|
| **A** Fixed Assets | | |
| Tangible Assets | 450 | Total of land, buildings, equipment etc. (less depreciation). Physical assets we can touch & count. |
| Investments | 75 | In associated and subsidiary businesses. |
| | 525 | |
| **B** Current Assets | | |
| Stocks | 100 | Lower of cost or market value for total of raw materials, work in progress and finished stock. |
| Debtors | 125 | Money owed by customers. |
| Cash | 25 | Year end total of cash in hand and at bank. |
| | 250 | |

| | | | |
|---|---|---|---|
| C | Creditors Falling due within 12 months | (110) | Total owing to suppliers plus outstanding taxation payable. |
| D | Net Current Assets (D=B−C) | 140 | Working Capital |
| E | Total Assets less Current Liabilities (E=A+D) | 665 | The total funds at work in the business i.e. what capital and reserves plus long-term loans have provided. |
| F | Creditors Falling due after 12 months | (125) | Money owed long-term e.g. debenture loans. |
| G | Provisions for Liabilities and Charges Deferred taxation | (105) | Technical liability if assets sold at book valuation (cost less capital depreciation) where this exceeds Inland Revenue valuation (cost less capital allowances for tax purposes) – see also footnotes to balance sheet. |
| H | (H = E−F−G) | 435 | |
| J | Capital and Reserves: Called up Share Capital | 180 | Money from sale of shares. |
| | Share Premium Account | 110 | If shares *used* above face value this is the funding received. |
| | Revaluation Reserve | 30 | Created when property revaluated above cost (the opposite of depreciation). |
| | Profit and Loss Account | 115 | Cumulative balance of retained profit from P&L Account over the years. |
| J | (J = H) | 435 | |

**XYZ Plc**
**Profit & Loss Account for year ended...**

"For year ended" the P&L Account is a summary of the whole year's business activity.

| | £000's | |
|---|---|---|
| • Turnover/Sales/Revenue/ Income | 750 | Alternative names for the amount of business done and invoiced (not necessarily paid). |
| Less: Cost of goods sold/ cost of sales: | | *Not* the cost of selling but rather the cost of providing what has been sold. what has been sold. |
| Materials | 120 | These costs all volume related (i.e. will alter in relation to level of sales & production |
| + Direct Labour | 140 | |
| + Direct Expenses | 40 | |
| | 300 | |
| • Gross Profit | 450 | Likely to change in line with amount of business undertaken. |
| Less: Indirect costs Admin. | 170 | These costs less variable/volume related, containing some 'fixed' elements. |
| Other overheads etc. | 160 | |
| | 330 | |

- Operating/Trading profit — 120 — Should reflect economies of scale when business increases.

  Less: Interest charges — 15 — Can be compared with dividends in terms of costs of raising finance through loans or shares.

- Profit before Tax — 105 — The most usual point of comparison for performance – year to year or with similar companies etc.

- Less: Tax — 20 — Corporation tax. Company account are presented *net* of VAT.

- Profit after Tax — 85

  Less: Dividends — 60 — Paid out of *taxed* profits. (Shareholders have income tax taken out of this amount in addition).

- Retained profit for year — 25 — Added to Reserves on the Balance Sheet.*

Note: *The P&L balance on the Balance Sheet will therefore increase by this amount from the previous year's balance.

Footnotes 1) Published accounts will also show figures for previous year, alongside the year being reported on for comparison. There will also be additional notes to the accounts to explain the basis on which the figures have been calculated.

2) Capital allowances: rather than allow judgements about rates of depreciation to alter taxable profit the Inland Revenue use capital allowances instead. As these are generally more generous in the effect they have in reducing tax to be paid, they may encourage investment in fixed assets (in order to keep the tax bill down) – to some degree.

## ABC Organisation

## Income & Expenditure Account for year ended...

"For year ended" = summary of the year's activity

Used for non-profit making organisations in place of P&L Account, to reveal any surplus or deficit arising from activities undertaken during the year.

£000's

**Income**

  Grants                          Listed individually according to purpose.

| | £000's | |
|---|---|---|
| Type 1 | 250 | |
| Type 2 | 100 | |
| Type 3 etc. | 150 | |
| | | 500 |

Other Income                    e.g. self-engendered sources of income

| | | |
|---|---|---|
| Sales | 130 | |
| Fees | 120 | |
| etc. | 250 | |
| | | 750 |

**Expenditure**

| | | |
|---|---:|---:|
| Type 1: Salaries and wages | 150 | |
| Overheads: | 95 | 245 |
| Type 2: Contractors fees | 75 | |
| Admin. costs | 30 | 105 |
| Type 3: Salaries and wages | 80 | |
| Overheads | 70 | 150 |
| Other admin/overheads costs (listed) | | 230 |
| | | 730 |
| Surplus (Deficit) of income over expenditure | | 20 |

Expenditure allocated or apportioned (split) by activity purpose, to enable comparison with funding – to ensure money used for purposes for which made available.

# Cash Flow Statement

This statement is new and replaces the former "Sources and Application of Funds" statement, which in itself is a relatively recent addition to published accounts – but much criticised for its complexity (in many small and medium sized companies the accountants themselves left it to the auditors to prepare – it was not much used for purposes of internal control within the business).

The Cash Flow Statement has a clearer structure perhaps, but it is not quite so easy to see where the figures have come from without the aid of supplementary notes to the accounts, so tracing out the whole picture can still be an involved process for the lay person.

It is perhaps a document of greater concern to financial specialists, interested in how funding (e.g. to aid growth of the business) has been raised and in what proportion internally from within the business versus the amount raised externally. If our interest is more focused on operational management issues, then this statement is of less concern to us (*for many the analysis of working capital changes on the balance sheet will give us a good enough 'handle' on the state of liquidity in the organisation, leaving the more technical issues concerning the mechanics of liquidity to the specialists*). In order to present a clear example of the concept of this statement, there is a danger of over simplification but the main principles should be apparent in the example on the next page.

## Cash Flow Statement ANO Company

£000's

- Net cash inflow from operating activities (see note)   27

- Returns on investments and servicing of finance

| | |
|---|---|
| Interest received | 5 |
| Interest paid | (8) |
| Dividends paid | (12) |

    Net cash outflow, investments and servicing finance   (15)

- Taxation paid   (10)

- Investing activities

| | |
|---|---|
| Purchase of fixed assets | (13) |
| Sale of investments | 5 |

    Net cash outflow, investing activities   (8)

- Financing

| | |
|---|---|
| Issue of shares | 20 |
| New Loans | 6 |
| Repayment of loans | (10) |

    Net cash inflow, financing   16

**INCREASE IN CASH AND CASH EQUIVALENTS**   10
(can be checked against change on balance sheet)

### Note to accounts

    Net cash inflow from operating activities

| | | |
|---|---|---|
| Operating profit | 21 | |
| Depreciation | 7 * | |
| Reduction in stocks | 2 | } being the year-to-year |
| Increase in debtors | (8) | } changes in the balance |
| Increase in creditors | 5 | } sheet figures |
| Total: | 27 | |

*added back because it was a non-cash deduction in arriving at operating profit

# Part Two:
# Financial planning and measuring trends

# 3 Financial Planning and Budgets

The budget should be no more than the next year's business plan expressed in financial terms. It therefore follows that the budget should not just be the proposed plan or "wish list" of an individual department, but something which is compatible with the plans for all parts of the organisation in order to achieve the desired result. If the department budget does not match the "big picture", it will have to change.

It may be helpful to consider the aggregate of all the individual budgets as a budgeted Profit & Loss Account (also resulting in a budgeted balance sheet). Although our budget proposals are frequently altered before they are finally approved – often leaving us to wonder if the budget is really "ours" in the end – it is as well to realise that however stringent the vetting process, it is a lot less painful than having to face corrective action mid-year as a result of having initially set off in a direction which we discover the business or enterprise cannot support.

If we can see the budget as next year's step in the business plan, this will help frame our thinking in the right way to begin with. The business plan is likely to be a document which sets the medium-term strategy within the context of the longer-term goals for the enterprise.

The longer-term elements are likely to exist in almost entirely narrative form, with little in the way of measurement (other than perhaps in relative terms e.g. to become "the best" in terms of . . .). It will be closely linked with the organisation's purpose and values. These elements can be valuable touch-stones for managers in terms of what decisions to take, what plans to commit to, when faced with change and uncertainty. "Mission", "Vision" and/or "Credos" (i.e. values in terms of beliefs) are likely to be the language of long-term corporate thinking.

The medium-term strategy and objectives are usually expressed in a mixture of narrative and key indicators or measures to be achieved, such as percentage sales growth or market share, return on net assets or capital employed etc. The financial measures may have been derived from an analysis of financial ratios drawn from the Balance Sheet, P & L and internal management accounts. A selection of possible ratios which might be reviewed is given on the following pages. They can be used with budget accounts, just as much as with actual results, to ensure that our collective plans in aggregate contain the possibility of delivering the required results.

# 4 Measuring trends with financial ratios

Financial ratios enable us to interpret more from the accounts of a business, by looking at the relationship of two sets of figures, than we would by looking at individual lines of numbers alone.

The term ratio is a loose generic term: results of these comparisons are rarely expressed as ratios in the form of, say, "4 to 1" or "5 to 1". Many of the results are expressed rather as percentages, or where a ratio might be expressed in its true mathematical sense, accountants use a shorthand version in stating the result as, say, "4" or "5" (the "to 1" part of the result being omitted). It is probably easier to see how this works in practice, so let's have a look at some examples.

## a) Ratios for assessing overall financial performance
If profits measure the increase in wealth of the business,

then we need to relate it to something in order to draw any conclusion about how good a result it is. A one million pound profit would hardly be adequate for a company the size of ICI but it would be fantastic, literally, for a local fish and chip shop.

One's first instinct might be to relate profit to sales (which we will look at in just a moment), but as a single overall measure, it may not be the best. Selling high volume but low margin goods may not produce very good profits as a percentage of sales but it may nonetheless provide a very worthwhile total profit through sheer volume of business (e.g. the "pile it high and sell it cheap" philosophy of the early days of Tesco).

A better single measure of financial performance is to relate profit to the amount of investment in the business; and by investment what we mean is that we need to consider all the funds a business has at its disposal: i.e. share capital reserves and (since it represents a source of retained funding even if it is not owned by the business) long-term creditors. This ratio is known as *return on capital employed* (ROCE) or alternatively *return on net assets* (RONA).

Since the capital employed is used to fund the net assets on the balance sheet, the figures used should be the same. However, there is some debate about whether or not the meaning "capital employed" extends as far as including long-term creditors; using the term "return on net assets" can at least avoid this argument. Also, if there is much change in capital employed/net assets from one year to the next, it may be preferable to base the calculation on the *average* capital employed rather than just the year end figure.

Our ratio is therefore:

Profits ÷ Average Net Assets × 100 = x%

Profits could be measured at any level e.g. gross, operating, retained, etc., but profits before tax is perhaps the best starting point for inter-firm or year to year comparisons, as it measures overall performance free of distortions caused by tax. What may be regarded as a satisfactory percentage return will vary according to the state of the economy and from industry to industry with their differing market conditions.

Our second ratio is to relate profit to sales or turnover: the *profit margin* ratio, which is:

Profits ÷ Sales × 100 = y%

Again, the percentage to expect will vary from industry to industry, from low margin, high unit volume to high margin, low unit volume for instance.

A third ratio 'squares the circle' between the first two. If we consider what *volume* of business is produced in relation to the amount invested in it, we end up looking at the ratio of sales to assets – known to accountants as the *rate of asset turnover*. This is:

Sales ÷ Net Assets = n times (for the period)

We can now sub-divide return on net assets (RONA) it being composed of the profit margin multiplied by the rate of asset turnover. If RONA results are unexpected or unsatisfactory, we can see whether it is caused by falling margins or falling volume (or a combination).

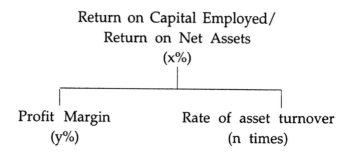

Return on Capital Employed/
Return on Net Assets
$(x\%)$

Profit Margin
$(y\%)$

Rate of asset turnover
(n times)

Therefore: $x = y \times n$

Other ratios can also be used to focus on particular parts of the business operation.

Many ratios can be a mixture of financial and non-financial ratios (e.g. profit per employee) and these are usually referred to as *management* ratios.

b) **Other noteworthy financial ratios we might consider are:**

- *Debtors ratio* which looks at what proportion of our sales are still outstanding for payment. Usually this is calculated as:

  Debtors ÷ Sales × 365* = Debtor Days

  – in order to reveal how long customers on average are taking to pay. (*Some organizations base the calculation on the number of working days rather than calendar days per year)
  Note: if the business is seasonal, it may be important to get the average rather than year end

figure for debtors to compare with annual sales. Otherwise, a Christmas Card manufacturer with a 31 December year end might not show up too well on this measure, for instance!

- *Stockturn ratio* which measures the number of times stock is turned over in the year:

    Cost of Sales ÷ Stocks = ? times

Again, average rather than closing figures (for stocks) may be more accurate if the business is seasonal.

Trends are more significant than interpreting a single result for this ratio. As stock is likely to be a mixture of raw materials, work in progress and finished stock in many situations, it would not often be meaningful to express the answer in stockholding days: (cost of sales ÷ stocks × 365).

- *Working Capital ratios* are used to make sure that the working capital is both sufficient and being used effectively.

The *current ratio* compares current assets and current liabilities (by dividing the former by the latter). Clearly we want enough in current assets to cover current liabilities, so we ought to see a result of over 1. If the result is over 2, then we might query whether the working capital is being used effectively – is it languishing in stock, debtors or cash and not circulating fast enough?

For some business, stock if slow moving may not be good cover for current liabilities (short-term creditors). The *quick ratio* (also known as the acid test) may be a better test of liquidity as it ignores stock, being:

(Debtors + Cash) ÷ current liabilities

Arguably the answer needs to be at least close to 1, but for some businesses (e.g. supermarkets) stock may be quicker to turn into cash, than debtors would be in other businesses – so the current ratio in such a case might be a more appropriate measure to use.

## Example of Ratio Calculations
## Using figures from XYZ plc Accounts (see pages 6-9)

**1  Return on Net Assets (RONA)**

$$\frac{\text{Profit before tax} = 105}{\text{Net Assets (taken as E)} = 465} \times 100 \quad = \underline{22.6\%}$$

**2  Profit Margin**

$$\frac{\text{Profit before tax} = 105}{\text{Turnover/Sales} = 750} \times 100 \quad = \underline{14.0\%}$$

**3  Rate of Asset Turnover**

$$\frac{\text{Turnover/Sales} \quad 750}{\text{Net Assets} \quad 465} = \underline{1.61 \text{ times}}$$

(Note: 14% Profit Margin × 1.61 Rate of Asset Turnover = 22.6% RONA)

**4  Debtor Days**

$$\frac{\text{Debtors} = 125}{\text{Turnover} = 750} \times 365 \quad = \underline{61 \text{ days}}$$

**5  Stockturn**

$$\frac{\text{Turnover} = 750}{\text{Stock} = 100} = \underline{7.5 \text{ times}}$$

**6  Current Ratio**

$$\frac{\text{Current Assets B} = 250}{\text{Current Liabilities} = 110} = \underline{2.27}$$

(creditors due within 12 months C)

**7  Quick Ratio/Acid Test of liquidity**

$$\frac{\text{Debtors + Cash}}{\text{Current Liabilities}} \quad \frac{125 + 25 = 150}{110} = \underline{1.36}$$

# Part Three:
# Budget preparation and use

# Seven Steps to Successful Budgeting

## Step 1   Define Objectives

We should now be ready to make a realistic assessment of what we need to achieve with our budget for the coming year, starting from a position where we do not see next year's budget simply as a perpetuation of what has gone before. The budget should help us focus on plans to improve performance and achieve goals or objectives for next year which represent stepping-stones within the longer-term business plan.

Because goals may change, we should record them. This is essential information for us to be able to look back upon, so that we know on which basis the budget was predicated. If the goals then change, then we can at least assess what compatible change in resources might be required and be in the best position to argue for any additions which might be necessary. As managers we know that one of the fundamental reasons for which our jobs exist, is the need not only to promote change pro-actively, but also to respond to those changes around us in terms of the competition, environment, technology, social factors, legislation etc. Moving goal-posts are the bane of many managers' lives – perhaps we can't (or shouldn't) stop it happening, but maybe we can manage the process.

We have now reviewed the first of "Seven Steps to Success" with budgeting, namely:

  1 Define Objectives

– and have begun to move to the second which is:

  2 Define Responsibility

The others, which will follow later, are:

  3 Gather the Facts
  4 Decide What to Submit
  5 Test and Check
  6 Win Approval
  7 Live with the Budget

and all seven steps are summarised again at the end of this handbook (Appendix 2).

# Step 2   Define Responsibility

In the same way that goals or objectives can change, in the same way so can our responsibilities and the accountability and authority that goes with them. For instance, supposing last year we were asked to take on responsibility for the photocopiers situated on the same floor as our department's offices, does this mean that this year all the maintenance contracts will be charged to our budget? It is important to check these changes out and ensure that the budget responsibility doesn't slip between two stools: starting off the financial year with unavoidable costs for which there is no budget would only make a mockery of attempts to budget all other items accurately.

We should also seek to clarify the boundaries of our control, particularly where authority limits are concerned. If we can sign off orders or invoices up to a certain amount of expenditure, where will amounts above that be charged and who holds the corresponding budget(s)?

If we wish to propose a change on our responsibilities, now is the time to do so, in order that the new budget can reflect such changes once agreed.

This step of checking and recording any shift in our responsibilities from year to year consumes little time in proportion to its possible importance.

# Step 3    Gather the Facts

When the request arrives to submit our budget proposals
for the next financial year in, say, five or six week's time,
how relieved we are that it doesn't have to be done this
week! In three or four week's time we haven't got nearly so
much work planned for ourselves as now, so there will be
a nice 'window of opportunity', to work on the budget.
Because we're only too glad to keep the budget preparation
task at arm's length for the time being, we delude
ourselves. We forget that between now and that 'window of
opportunity' all sorts of other commitments will arise and,
if not careful, we will find ourselves as rushed as ever to
put the budget together by the required deadline. Then if
we don't do a very good job of predicting our expenditure
(or income), we can at least console ourselves with the
thought that it was only lack of time and pressure of other
work rather than our lack of ability that reduced us to this
sorry plight.

So let's get rid of this myth that budgeting is difficult for
once and for all. The first thing to recognise is that there is
no magic secret to getting it right – no "one-way" of preparing a budget that guarantees success. A budgetary
control system is like an organisation's fingerprint – they all
vary even though we can basically recognise what they are.
If there is something that looks odd in the way the budgets
are put together or reported on (in terms of actuals and
variances) the first thing we should do is *ask* about it – there
may be quite a few other managers in the organisation who
would secretly like to know, but also didn't realise that it
was not something everyone in business everywhere was
supposed to know!

The next thing we need to do if we are determined to become skilled at budgeting is to be systematic about the way we apply our common sense – which will be the foundation of our success with budgets far more than any grasp we have of the workings of finance, however helpful that may be.

So, to return to that moment when the request to prepare the budget arrives. If we have kept an updated record of our objectives and responsibilities as indicated in steps one and two, then the next things that we should *immediately* do are:

a) Break down the budget task into a number of sub-tasks such as:

- Collect latest information on variances for the current year to date and predict year end position (by scaling pro-rata and adjusting for specific known factors which require special attention).
- Reviewing changes in operation for next year arising from the objectives set for it and how this will affect revenue and/or costs.
- Applying any necessary adjustments to the likely (annual) figures to be used in next year's budget for:-
  - inflation (possibly by category rather than separately for each item)
  - changes in activity level in line with any central policy guidance from the finance function on these factors.
- Once proposed annual figures have been arrived at, cross-casting expenditure codes and monthly totals to check the overall figures for the year look sensible – both in terms of what we need and what we think will be acceptable. (See also step 5 which follows).

b) Plan time for each of these sub-tasks in the diary on different days – we can't expect to do them all at once. Even if the boss (or other circumstance) dictates we can't get to that task on the appointed day, at least the need to control the slippage will be obvious and if we haven't planned the tasks back-to-back we stand a good chance of maintaining our overall timetable (which should allow a few days contingency between the completion and submission dates).

c) If necessary, set up meetings with other budget holders in cases where changes we might be contemplating have budget consequences for them – or vica versa. This will be particularly important where there are shared resources between departments which come into the budget review.

d) Think about how we can involve others in the budget preparation – if we want the members of the team to be committed to achieving what it asks for, it is vital that they do not feel it is imposed and therefore only someone else's problem (ours) when it risks failing.

Whilst we may worry about raised expectations which might not be met at the budget approval stage, it is at least better for the team to know that unpopular decisions were not taken in ignorance (see also step 6).

e) If we can't action the collection of current status information as in the first point under item (a) above straight away – delegate the job to someone else. It is vital that when we sit down for the first hour or two's real work on the budget, that we don't have to fritter it away by having to collect the information we need to start with because it wasn't to hand. This could also apply to the collection of data or guidelines about inflation forecasts or activity levels (e.g. anticipated changes in sales &/or production) if this has not already been spelt out centrally by the finance function on the budget preparation request.

# Step 4   Decide What to Submit

The chances are that when we have arrived at some preliminary annual totals which suggest themselves (on the basis of starting from this year's expected out-turn plus the various changes we envisage), these won't look or feel quite "right". Either we will feel that the budget would look inadequate for the size of the task in front of us and the uncertainties and risks attached to it, or we will feel that seeking approval for a budget of this size would be crying for the moon.

We should not brush aside our feelings in the face of cold logic – they are just as important to the budget process as our logical deductions if we are to do the best we can and do justice to our position as a budget holder. We should examine our feelings and see if we can establish the causes of our unease. Then we can use our analytical abilities to see what further adjustments are necessary to get to a set of figures with which we feel comfortable.

The figures we seek to submit may therefore be a mixture of cold facts, hunches and "guesstimates" – all are valid and at times useful in the process of deciding what to submit. Above all, however, we must *record* (even if only for own use) how we got to these figures. The supporting detail can be in narrative form just as much as figures – keep a note of the arguments involved. No matter how imprecise the science of arriving at a figure, if we know that we have tried to weigh it up from every angle and can only pick some tenuous basis for our chosen guess, we should not be shy about it. If the figure is challenged at the approval stage and we can show how we got to the figure, we can always ask for ideas on a more informed way of arriving at the answer – if there isn't one, then ours is that much harder to argue against. If there is a better way, we can adopt it.

Keeping what we might call an "audit trail" of how the decisions were taken on what to submit for the budget also had advantages after the approval stage too. When we are using the budget to control expenditure and there are unexpected variances, it can be useful to check on the basis on which the budget figure was set. If the circumstances have clearly changed from those on which the budget was set and agreed, the variance can be explained (not that this will excuse us from remedial action if necessary – see step seven: 'Living with the Budget').

When it is difficult to predict what figures are required for a sensible budget, the question of how to deal with *contingencies* arises. What will be acceptable may well be determined by studying the organisation culture. In some organisations, the culture may be one of allowing absolutely no safety factor and the budget can become more of a target to aim for (as opposed to a standard, the achievement of which can be relied on under normal circumstances). In such cases it is to be hoped that a central contingency fund is created by the organisation – although its existence is unlikely to be disclosed to individual budget-holders. In other organisations, prudence may rule and budgets would not be thought sensible unless some (but not lavish) contingency were present – either through reasonable "rounding up" to slightly higher figures or by inclusion of a miscellaneous or sundries account as cover for the unexpected (as well as covering those small or infrequent items of expenditure not large enough to justify an account category coding of their own). If in doubt about how to handle the accuracy/contingency factor – ask questions, but listen to the message behind the words about the culture and what it says about how tightly the budget hould be drawn (the strength of the message may vary from year to year within the prevailing organisation culture).

Where there are questions of fluctuating activity or demand levels from month to month, these are dealt with by the techniques of either profiling or flexible budgeting, which are dealt with in step 5 which follows. However, it will still be necessary to look first at the expected annual totals in activity and cost terms in order to get a picture of how well the budget and its underlying assumptions are matched with those of other functions in the organisation. Limits on year to year increases in the budget and/or the levels of activity to budget for, should have been amongst the information either supplied to, or sought out by, us in step 3 – gathering the facts. (Although, as we will see later, this may be re-appraised on an organisation-wide basis in step 6 – the approval stage).

From step 3 also you may remember that we should have been giving some thought as to how to involve our staff in the budgeting process. We should now be putting those thoughts into action. People closest to the problems presented by their work often have the best ideas about how improvements could be achieved. If these ideas are built into the budget submission, then the commitment to making it work in practice will be very high.

If we envisage changed ways of working which might affect or influence other parts of the organisation, then it is to our advantage to also involve peer group managers of other interested departments in an early stage of the development of our plans. Quite apart from any useful ideas they may have, their support could be crucial when we get to the budget approval stage.

# Example of Pro Forma
# For Budget Preparation

| Department Name: | | | | Technical Services | Dept. No. 010 |
|---|---|---|---|---|---|
| Last Year | This Year | | | Expenditure | Next |
| Actual | Budget to date | Actual to date | Projected year end | Code Description | Year Proposed |
| | | | | **Wages & Salaries**<br>010100 Hourly paid<br>010120 Monthly paid<br><br>**Transport etc.**<br>010220 Company cars<br>010221 Fuel costs<br>010223 Tyres & repairs<br>010240 Rail & other fares<br><br>**Stationery**<br>010500 Materials<br>010530 Photocopier costs<br><br>**Central charges**<br>010900 Management charges<br>010700 Space/Heat/Light<br>010880 Information systems<br>010680 Maintenance<br>                Recharges | |
| | | | | **Total** | |

Note: • Comparison of budget and actual for year to date helps ensure that the projected year end figures look realistic. See "Example of Budget Variance Report" on page 54 for likely source data for making this projection.

• Comparing last year, this year (projected) and next year (proposed) may be useful for examining the nature of any trends.

# Step 5    Test and Check

Simple spread-sheet software takes much of the grind out of this stage. As soon as we break down the annual amounts we have decided to go for in the previous stage into monthly amounts, the cross-costing becomes automatic and any subsequent changes are immediately reflected in the departmental totals for the month and the annual totals by account code.

As has been mentioned, not all annual totals should be divided equally between the months. Here are some of the considerations.

(i)     Not all months are the same length in terms of working days (being affected by the number of weekends, bank holidays etc.) let alone calendar length. Some organisations seek to mitigate this by having, for instance, 13 accounting periods of 4 weeks each in the year, or balancing the quarters with "months" of 4, 4 & 5 weeks in each quarter.

(ii)    If either costs or levels of activity are affected by the amount of staff holidays, we will need to allow for this, if predictable.

(iii)   The work-pattern may well be seasonal in terms of peaks and troughs in some organisations because of the nature of their products or services.

(iv)    Some expenditure may be difficult to predict in terms of the month in which it will occur e.g. if our department is large enough to assume some notional turnover of staff is likely in the year, in which month do we put the proposed budget for recruitment cost?

(Assuming that is charged to us and not covered within the Personnel budget). Do we put in an amount in the likely month(s) or spread it evenly?

(v)   Where production levels are sales driven, it will not be sensible to say what production costs are likely to be until the actual level of demand is known.

Points (i), (ii) and (iii) are covered by *"profiling"* or *"calendarisation"*, which is nothing more than flexing the monthly figures according to some characteristic such as the number of actual working days in the month or following the historical profile of previous years.

Point (iv) is dealt with according to the type of expenditure involved and our forecasting or clairvoyant abilities! If in doubt, it is best to spread the budget evenly, so that even if there is no actual expenditure of this type in any month, it is a reminder that a sum has been budgeted, the adequacy of which may have to be judged finally at the year end. Indeed in order to avoid fluctuations in monthly variances, the unused budget can be a useful reminder of the possible need to make a provision for expenditure not yet charged by means of an *accrual*.

Point (v) involves *flexible budgeting* using unit standard costs for direct expenditure. Direct costs are those which can be charged directly to the product, because we know how much goes into each unit (e.g. raw materials, direct labour, component cost, packaging etc.) and the total bill each month for usage of these items will vary according to the level of production. By contrast, overheads will be more stable (often with a significant proportion of fixed costs unaffected by changes in volume or activity levels).

Actual production costs are therefore compared with the standard allowance for the direct costs for the volume or level of production that has taken place. The management accounting function will be able to analyse variances into price, efficiency and (in the case of overhead recovery) volume. The production manager is usually left with having to establish a conventional budget for the department's own "overhead" expenses, whereas standard cost allowances will be derived within the accounting function.

Once all the budget proposals are set out, we not only need to check that they conform with policy guidelines in terms of year on year increase etc., but also that we feel comfortable with the figures in the way that they "stack up". Can we justify them? Are we prepared to live with them?

We need to resist being carried away with warm feelings just because we have completed the preparatory work and produced something apparently acceptable to others. It is easy to be a hero one day a year, and then find we are found wanting the other 364 because we didn't put forward a budget which was workable in terms of meeting the real needs of our department. If we are to put forward proposals which challenge the parameters we were expected to work within, then we need to have looked at all possible angles in being able to demonstrate our case.

Sometimes we can clear away a lot of preconceptions (not least our own) about how much the provision of a service should cost by adopting an approach known as *"Zero Based Budgeting"*. This discipline requires each budget holder to justify his/her proposed budget as if it were a totally new proposal i.e. we have to start from scratch or a "zero base".

Once we have clarified the business objective for which the budget is required, we then have to look at the most cost-efficient way of achieving this, rather than perpetuating existing structures and ways of working. It is the sort of approach which has helped accelerate the trend towards out-sourcing services (such as security, catering, payroll preparation etc.) which are not core to the enterprise – leaving top management more free to concentrate their expertise on those distinctive activities which mark out the organisation's niche in the market place.

Zero Based Budgeting is not only consistent with this philosophy but also the drive towards shorter, flatter hierarchies, which become more possible with the reduced span of control of functions directly managed. However, if the enthusiasm for Zero Based Budgeting is very strong, it may be worth considering whether there might be some merit in working round the organisation over, say a three, four or five year time span on a rolling basis. By concentrating on one major aspect of the business each year, radical proposals can be more thoroughly investigated and evaluated. If everything is changing at once there is a chance that something which with hindsight always seems to be more significant than we would have imagined initially, slips between the cracks of the new organisation which is being created. The counter-argument is, obviously, that unless we adopt this radical approach on a total basis it is difficult to take a holistic approach to organisation design. Perhaps we could have the best of both ways of looking at this. This would comprise a year one organisation-wide review using Zero Budgeting followed by phased implementation over, say, years one, two and three. Thereafter each section of the business could adopt the zero-based discipline maybe once every four years – a different section of the business being up for review on this basis each year.

# Step 6  Win Approval

If we have adopted much of what has gone before in the previous stages of preparation of our budget, we should now be well prepared and well placed to win approval for our proposals, if that is at all possible.

We should make it easy for those to whom we present to approve our submissions. This means ensuring that we adopt standard form layouts, codings of expenditure categories (and income ones, too if these feature in our budget) and adoption of house style for setting out any supporting information. Regardless of whether we make a formal presentation or only a written submission, the key features of our budget strategy should be listed in some form of "executive summary". At a face-to-face presentation, taking the notes of our "audit trail" for arriving at our decisions on what to submit will be invaluable. If it is only a written submission, we have to make a decision about the appropriate level of supporting detail to be given in explaining how particular figures were arrived at.

Unless there is a procedure which dictates otherwise, we should be trying this out with our boss first, before the proposals go the Finance function or Budget Review Committee (see diagram on page 52). Seeking formal approval from our boss does not begin at this stage – we should have been keeping our boss informed about our ideas as they have been formulated. Not only might he or she have some valuable input to the process, but early discussion is also part of the 'selling' process. Nor should we keep the Finance department at arms length while we are working on our proposals if we have been able to establish good working relationships.

Prior to the actual submission or presentation it may be wise to try out or 'rehearse' the proposals with a team member in the department – particularly if there has been someone who has been helping us with the task (hopefully as part of their own development as much as making the task less onerous for ourselves by delegation).

Despite all this, we should not be surprised if approval is not immediate! Often after much pressure to achieve a submission deadline, all goes quiet for several weeks and it feels like all our hard work has disappeared into a "black hole". Then our proposals reappear either with alterations in place or instructions to take x% off certain figures (or add y% more income) – and all this despite exhortations, before the budget round started, that this year needed to be different with budgeting really becoming a "bottom up" process, and not imposed from the top, enabling us to really "own" our budgets!

If all this sounds horribly familiar, then we may need to:

• remember that there is no point in approving budgets which do not make an integrated plan for the right results. The delay in approval may have been for the need not only to produce budgeted P & L and Balance Sheet statements, but also to 'test' these with some of the Financial Ratios referred to earlier. Either this process, or the something that has come to light in putting together the budgets themselves, may have revealed that some of the underlying policy assumptions we started with are not achievable – perhaps the forecast limiting factor of, say, sales or production capacity which determined the guidelines for everyone else is now seen differently.

# Budget Approval Process: Information & Reporting Flow

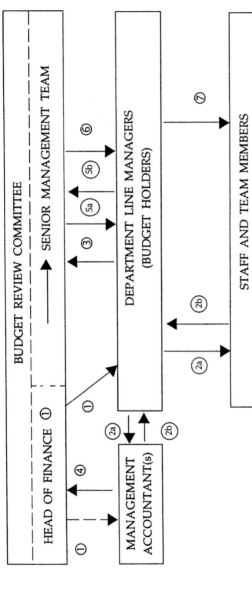

① = Budget preparation requests issued with required timetable/deadlines and policy guidelines e.g. growth &/or inflation assumptions

② = a) consultation for ideas & b) feedback for consideration

③ = Proposed budget submitted

④ = Critique submitted from accounts/finance to support budget review

⑤ = a) Post review amendments requested, in order to make all budget mutually compatible with each other and corporate plan
b) Counter proposals resolved

⑥ = Approval

⑦ = Budget responsibility shared with team, to clarify accountabilities and secure commitment to approved budget

- make a more closely-argued re-submission of our budget if we still believe our proposals were correct.

- be philosophical if we ultimately cannot win the day. Perhaps either our arguments were not good enough, we are too close to the implications to be objective, we cannot expect to "win" if we have not been skilful enough or well enough prepared, or maybe those at the top really do know best because they have the "big picture".

- sell the approved budget to our staff. If we have the right (and duty) to have fought as well as we can for the budget we have acquired, then we clearly have the duty to secure the commitment of our team to achieving to what is required. This may not be easy – particularly if their aspirations were for something more favourable (and given that we have tried to incorporate their ideas in what was submitted) – but if leadership were that easy then the need for our jobs to exist might be questionable! Of course some decisions the team may not agree with, but as has been previously stated, in the long run these may be easier to accept if the team feels it has at least been consulted and knows the final decisions were eventually reached without ignorance of its points of view and concerns. It goes without saying that we can't expect the team to take the budget seriously unless we demonstrate our commitment to it first.

# Step 7   Live with the Budget

From the foregoing it is clear that how we handle the approval stage will have much to do with how well the budget is accepted as a real (and, if not too demanding, a helpful) discipline to work within.

No matter how carefully the budget has been framed, there will be variances. Just how far we will be held to account for absolutely any and every variance and have to justify them, may depend on how pro-active we are about reporting on the situation. If we can demonstrate that we quickly assess not only causes of major variances (favourable as well on adverse!) but also state how we propose to bring things back on course where necessary, then our superiors are likely to feel confident that they can leave the detail to us. If we fail to demonstrate we are in control, and reports and commentaries on the published variances do not come from us until asked for, the more gruelling our cross-examination is likely to be.

Just because we may be logging a series of favourable variances does not mean we can automatically assume all is well. For instance, is it possible that some charges we could have expected to see have been charged to another cost or profit centre, due to coding error(s)? We need to be on top of costs sufficiently to have a pretty good idea of what to expect before the monthly variance statement is issued (if we have developed a good relationship with the Finance department through our pro-active approach, unusual variances may even be checked out with us before the variance statements are finalised and published).

budget statements, we may have a false view of our true position. In some systems, particularly where the over-riding financial controls are focused on cash flow, invoices may not appear on our expense statements until they are actually paid (which could be 60 to 80 days after the invoice has been received!). If the focus is on profit, then the invoice may be posted when received and approved (checked); but even this, in some cases, could be some time after the goods or services (to which the invoice relates) have been received. Hence we need to keep a rough tally of what we believe the position truly to be, to check our budget reports against.

If the organisation is one which is directly or indirectly funded by another (e.g. government funded), then the concern may be more about how much money is uncommitted and still available for use before the year end, when unspent balances will be lost. In these circumstances, reporting of actual versus budget spending may be on the basis of commitment (e.g. orders placed) rather than cash flow. If there is a danger of some account headings being underspent, where others could easily be overspent because plans are more advanced, then a process known as "*virement*" may operate. This enables the unspent balances to be used where they are required elsewhere, with perhaps a reversal of the budget allocation in the following financial period.

If we are able to establish a pattern of variances which look like persisting, then we may be in a position to *forecast* the future pattern of performance against budget. The further we get through the financial year, the more our forecasts will be requested and begin to take the place of the original budget itself as the yardstick against which we will be

**Example of Budget Variance Report**

**Month 6: October    Technical Services Department**                        **Dept. No. 010**

Expense Category                 Current Month              Year to Date              Last year

| Code | Description | Budget | Actual | Variance | | Budget | Actual | Variance | | Actual to date |
|---|---|---|---|---|---|---|---|---|---|---|
| | **Wages & Salaries** | | | | | | | | | |
| 010100 | Hourly Paid (inc. overtime) | 6,800 | 7,030 | (230) | (3%) | 37,600 | 38,875 | (1275) | (3%) | 34,992 |
| 010120 | Monthly Paid | 8,700 | 8,590 | 110 | 1% | 52,200 | 51,540 | 660 | 1% | 50.847 |
| | **Transport etc.** | | | | | | | | | |
| 010220 | Company car leases | 675 | 687 | (12) | (2%) | 4,050 | 4,122 | (72) | (2%) | 2,430 |
| 010221 | Fuel costs | 260 | 243 | 17 | 7% | 1,490 | 1,538 | (48) | (3%) | 983 |
| 010223 | Tyres and repairs | 50 | – | 50 | 100% | 300 | 221 | 79 | 26% | 217 |
| 010240 | Rail, Taxi, Plane etc. | 175 | 349 | (174) | (99%) | 1,050 | 1,104 | (54) | (5%) | 1,071 |
| | **Stationery** | | | | | | | | | |
| 010500 | Materials | 45 | 53 | (8) | (18%) | 270 | 33 | (66) | (24%) | 303 |
| 010530 | Photocopier costs | 120 | 108 | 12 | 10% | 720 | 594 | 126 | 18% | 576 |
| | **Central charges** | | | | | | | | | |
| 010900 | Management charge | 2,500 | 2,375 | 125 | 5% | 15,000 | 14,15 | 850 | 6% | 13,800 |
| 010700 | Space/heat/light | 1,105 | 1,060 | 45 | 4% | 6,540 | 6,320 | 22 | 03% | 6,420 |
| 010880 | Information systems | 1,340 | 1,427 | (87) | (6%) | 8,040 | 8,29 | (254) | (3%) | 7,639 |
| 010680 | Maintenance recharges | 175 | 133 | 42 | 24% | 1,050 | 869 | 181 | 17% | 1,002 |
| | **Total** | 21,945 | 22,055 | (110) | (1%) | 129,310 | 127,963 | 347 | 0% | 120,280 |

Points to note:
- VARIANCES: ( ) = ADVERSE (not true of all systems). Variances could be shown as + or − instead.
- Expense code is an example of a mixture of department code (010) and expense category (3 digit with generic groupings)
- Overtime is often shown as a separate line – how far is it cause of overspend in hourly paid wages above?
- Some variance reports may also display actual and budgeted headcount information
- INTERPRETATION: Look for trends – is the % variance for the current month similar to the % year to date?

    What is more significant for investigation – the % variance or the size of the variance in £?

    Does the comparison with this time last year suggest anything?

measured. There may be a temptation to forecast on the basis of an apparently established trend (particularly if favourable) without understanding it in detail. This should be resisted. By preparing forecasts, we are not only effectively re-budgeting the remainder of this financial year, but also establishing the basic position from which we might expect to develop next year's budget. Some effort to understand the present situation will more than repay itself in the future. Not that our efforts with the present should be limited to understanding. We must avoid "paralysis by analysis" – we need to develop action plans to both correct and control adverse variances and exploit or maximise favourable ones.

It is not unusual to feel that if actual results always vary from the budget because circumstances change, why bother to plan in this way? The answer is to see the budget as something to steer by – we may not be able to follow it exactly, but by measuring how far we deviate from it we know where we are. Even if where we are is in fact the best or most logical place to be, using the budget (almost as a navigation aid) helps us define that position. Perhaps Eisenhower summed it up most succinctly when he said of plans of all sorts (in the context of the D-Day landings I believe) "the plan is nothing . . .planning is everything". Hopefully the seven stages we have been through helps us to see that the value of the budgeting as a process is what matters – not just the listing of columns of figures at the end.

# 6

# Capital Budgets

Our seven steps have so far related to Revenue Budgets – so called to firstly distinguish them from budgets which deal with capital expenditure and secondly because they deal with budgets which are either about income (i.e. revenue) or costs incurred in creating and to be charged against revenue.

Capital expenditure relates to fixed assets which remain in the business over, and for the benefit of, many revenue periods. Therefore it is only their depreciation charges not their total cost which will appear in the P & L account for any one year. Depreciation spreads that total cost over the period of years which benefit from use of the asset. Whether or not depreciation will be charged on the revenue budget of the department holding or using the asset, varies from organisation to organisation – some like to control it in a central fixed overhead budget, others prefer to charge it out to the departments concerned.

The Capital Budget will, (like revenue budgets, as we have seen,) be derived in part from the Business Plan. Some capital expenditure becomes inevitable as the consequence of having decided on certain business objectives and where such expenditure can be identified, it is simple to budget for. Over and above allowing for such specific items/plans, the capital budget will almost certainly include an element or allowance for "discretionary spend", usually of a sort to be justified on the basis of cost reduction or increased revenue which should result. There also may be additional sums for other categories such as "regulatory" to cover compliance with legislation, Health and Safety requirements etc.

In the case of capital expenditure which has to be justified on the basis of savings or benefits, different proposals will be put forward during the year as and when they are identified and will therefore be competing with other schemes for whatever funds are available in the Capital Budget. In order to rank the comparative viability of different proposals, the following methods of justification are in common use.

## A: Pay Back Period
– which simply states how long it takes for the £ benefits to add up to the capital outlay required at the start. It is an easy-to-use calculation but takes no account of how beneficial the project is after pay-back has been achieved. It is not uncommon for proposals to need to pay for themselves in 2+ years to stand a chance of approval so far as discretionary capital spending is concerned.

# B: Return on Capital or Return on Investment

– sometimes also referred to as average rate of return. With this method, benefits over the length of the project or practical time horizon for forecasting purposes (say 5 years) are averaged as an annual figure, which is then expressed as a percentage of the outlay. Whilst this method can look over the whole life of the project, it does not distinguish between the value of early or later benefits. Pound for pound, early returns or benefits are in reality more valuable as they are available for reinvestment sooner.

As both methods A and B are simple, they may be used together, particularly at the stage of trying to make some preliminary assessment or comparison between different schemes to meet the same business objective. However, being simple, they are easy to manipulate to give the result required to secure approval. In part, this might be a reason why short pay-back/high return on capital figures are sought – as protection against over-optimistic projections! Post-implementation audits of capital expenditure projects may have difficulty in identifying the originally forecast benefits – particularly if they included 'notional' benefits.

Notional benefits are not easy to quantify accurately, even if they are to be recognised in the financial benefits at all. Suppose we wish to justify the purchase of some new word-processors and software. Amongst the benefits we might list a saving of, say, 1½ hours per day of secretarial time. But will that "saving" actually materialise in cash/profit terms? Perhaps not unless we actually employ a secretary for less time (unlikely), although we could argue that we could transfer more of our own work to fill the released capacity – which might result in our being able to produce even greater financial benefits ourselves (e.g. more customer contact time and more business!)

## C: Discounted Cash Flow

– this technique does not overcome all the problems, but its introduction into an organisation often produces a sudden rush of honesty amongst people submitting capital expenditure requests – if only because it looks sufficiently complex that trying to fiddle the answers might catch one out!

However, the great strength of this approach is that it does put a value on the timing of cash flows. It assumes that the longer we have to wait for future benefits, the less they are worth pound for pound in today's money compared with earlier inflows or the initial capital outflow. A pound in the future is worth less to us than a pound today because of the interest the latter earns in the meantime. It is rather like compound interest in reverse, with each succeeding year's projected returns or benefits being more heavily discounted than the preceding one.

There are two ways of using the technique (see also worked example which follows):

(i) *Net Present Value*
With this method, the discounted future benefits over the life of the project are totalled up and the initial outlay deducted, to leave the Net Present Value (NPV) of the proposal. The discount rate to be used is

normally set for the organisation by the finance function, usually by reference to prevailing interest rate structures (e.g. cost of overdraft) or on the basis of the return on net assets (RONA) being achieved in the business at present (on an opportunity cost basis, presumably any funds diverted from the business at large to a specific purpose should at least match this). The scheme with the highest NPV is the one which would be favoured.

(ii) *Internal Rate of Return*
This method requires us to find out what discount rate will reduce the NPV to exactly zero. This rate is then the Internal Rate of Return (IRR) and the higher the IRR the more attractive the proposition becomes. This method is even more difficult to handle "longhand" or manually than the NPV method because it requires a lot of trial and error with different discount factors to get the NPV to precisely zero.

As one might expect, there are simple P.C. programmes which can handle the discounted cash flow calculations (both methods) for us – there are even programmable calculators which will do them!

At the end of the day, Capital Investment Appraisal methods are only designed to give us a ranking of the proposals in order to assist decision making. Passing the test of a sophisticated technique does not make the decision any more sound than the premises on which the original benefit calculations are founded. Even adding additional percentages to the discount factor in the NPV method according to the perceived level of risk (which results in a mixed risk and time-weighted calculation anyway) does not make it "safe". Whatever the chances were of the risk becoming fact are still the same, even if we have made it harder for the project to be approved.

It is always possible that compelling commercial arguments (e.g. helping to meet a market need which brings spin-off customer-loyalty to other parts of the business) may outweigh what can easily be measured financially; but if we can present a case which is both commercially and financially attractive in investment appraisal terms, then we really are on to a winner in securing the funding required.

# Example of Capital Investment Appraisal Techniques

Assume we have a proposal to spend £150k (in year 0) on, say, upgrading desk top computing in the office and that the benefits have been assessed as follows:

| | | |
|---|---|---|
| Year 1 | £ 30K | (early days) |
| Year 2 | 90 K | (project really into its stride) |
| Year 3 | 60 K | (benefits tailing off) |
| Year 4 | 30 K | (benefits coming to an end) |

**Pay Back Calculation**

$$\text{Benefits years 1 \& 2} = £120K$$
$$+ \text{½ year} = \underline{\quad 30K\quad}$$
$$150K \quad (= \text{outlay})$$

∴ Pay-back period = <u>2½ years</u>

**Return on capital (ROI)**

Benefits over 4 years total £210K

∴ average per annum is 52.5K

Average rate of return on capital investment is therefore:

$$\frac{£52.5K}{£150K \text{ outlay}} \times 100 = \underline{35\%}$$

## Discounted Cash Flow

### (i) Net Present Value

Assume we have been told to use a 12% discount rate, resulting in the Discount Factors (DF) below:

DF*

| | | | |
|---|---|---|---|
| Yr. 1 benefits £30K × 0.893 | = | £26,790 |
| 2 | 90K × 0.797 | = | 71,730 |
| 3 | 60K × 0.712 | = | 42,720 |
| 4 | 30K × 0.636 | = | 19,080 |
| | | | £160,320 |

less outlay  150,000  (Year 0)

Net Present Value £10,320

*The discount factor can be looked up in discount tables as on page 67 – or they can be calculated as follows:

- Enter the number 1 in calculator
- Divide by 1 plus the percentage discount rate required, thus:

    10% DF  =  divisor of 1.10 (i.e. 1 + 10%)

    11% DF  =                         1.11

    12% DF  =                         1.12

    etc.

  The result is the DF for year 1

  (in the example above, 1 ÷ 1.12 = 0.893, being the figure which, when increased by 12% over the year would bring us back to 1).
- Record the year 1 discount factor (e.g. 0.893) but leave it in the calculator. Divide by the required divisor (e.g. 1.12) and record the result (e.g. 0.797) as the year 2 discount factor.
- Repeat the previous step for as many subsequent years for which a discount factor is required.

## (ii) Internal Rate of Return

Not suitable for manual or "long-hand" calculations. We are trying to find the rate of return (compound) we would have to earn before an alternative investment would be equally attractive as the proposed project. This equates to a discount factor which, if used in the above calculation, would reduce the NPV to exactly zero. By trial and error (in the absence of suitable software) this can be found to be just over 15%.

# Discount/Present Value Factors

Present value of £1 to be received in one payment at the
end of a given number of years
Discount rates of 10% to 18%

| Future | Percentage rate of Discount | | | | | | | | |
|--------|-------|-------|-------|-------|-------|-------|-------|-------|-------|
| Years | 10 | 11 | 12 | 13 | 14 | 15 | 16 | 17 | 18 |
| 1 | 0.909 | 0.901 | 0.893 | 0.885 | 0.877 | 0.870 | 0.862 | 0.855 | 0.847 |
| 2 | 0.826 | 0.812 | 0.797 | 0.783 | 0.769 | 0.756 | 0.743 | 0.731 | 0.718 |
| 3 | 0.751 | 0.731 | 0.712 | 0.693 | 0.675 | 0.658 | 0.641 | 0.624 | 0.609 |
| 4 | 0.683 | 0.659 | 0.636 | 0.613 | 0.592 | 0.572 | 0.552 | 0.534 | 0.516 |
| 5 | 0.621 | 0.593 | 0.567 | 0.543 | 0.519 | 0.497 | 0.476 | 0.456 | 0.437 |
| 6 | 0.564 | 0.535 | 0.507 | 0.480 | 0.456 | 0.432 | 0.410 | 0.390 | 0.370 |
| 7 | 0.513 | 0.482 | 0.452 | 0.425 | 0.400 | 0.376 | 0.354 | 0.333 | 0.314 |
| 8 | 0.467 | 0.434 | 0.404 | 0.376 | 0.351 | 0.327 | 0.305 | 0.285 | 0.266 |
| 9 | 0.424 | 0.391 | 0.361 | 0.333 | 0.308 | 0.284 | 0.263 | 0.243 | 0.225 |
| 10 | 0.386 | 0.352 | 0.322 | 0.295 | 0.270 | 0.247 | 0.227 | 0.208 | 0.191 |
| 11 | 0.350 | 0.317 | 0.287 | 0.261 | 0.237 | 0.215 | 0.195 | 0.178 | 0.162 |
| 12 | 0.319 | 0.286 | 0.257 | 0.231 | 0.208 | 0.187 | 0.168 | 0.152 | 0.137 |
| 13 | 0.290 | 0.258 | 0.229 | 0.204 | 0.182 | 0.163 | 0.145 | 0.130 | 0.116 |
| 14 | 0.263 | 0.232 | 0.205 | 0.181 | 0.160 | 0.141 | 0.125 | 0.111 | 0.099 |
| 15 | 0.239 | 0.209 | 0.183 | 0.160 | 0.140 | 0.123 | 0.108 | 0.095 | 0.084 |
| 16 | 0.218 | 0.188 | 0.163 | 0.141 | 0.123 | 0.107 | 0.093 | 0.081 | 0.071 |
| 17 | 0.198 | 0.170 | 0.146 | 0.125 | 0.108 | 0.093 | 0.080 | 0.069 | 0.060 |
| 18 | 0.180 | 0.153 | 0.130 | 0.111 | 0.095 | 0.081 | 0.069 | 0.059 | 0.051 |
| 19 | 0.164 | 0.138 | 0.116 | 0.098 | 0.083 | 0.070 | 0.060 | 0.051 | 0.043 |
| 20 | 0.149 | 0.124 | 0.104 | 0.087 | 0.073 | 0.061 | 0.051 | 0.043 | 0.037 |
| 21 | 0.135 | 0.112 | 0.093 | 0.077 | 0.064 | 0.053 | 0.044 | 0.037 | 0.031 |
| 22 | 0.123 | 0.101 | 0.083 | 0.068 | 0.056 | 0.046 | 0.038 | 0.032 | 0.026 |
| 23 | 0.112 | 0.091 | 0.074 | 0.060 | 0.049 | 0.040 | 0.033 | 0.027 | 0.022 |
| 24 | 0.102 | 0.082 | 0.066 | 0.053 | 0.043 | 0.035 | 0.028 | 0.023 | 0.019 |
| 25 | 0.092 | 0.074 | 0.059 | 0.047 | 0.038 | 0.030 | 0.024 | 0.020 | 0.016 |
| 30 | 0.057 | 0.044 | 0.033 | 0.026 | 0.020 | 0.015 | 0.012 | 0.009 | 0.007 |
| 35 | 0.036 | 0.026 | 0.019 | 0.014 | 0.010 | 0.008 | 0.006 | 0.004 | 0.003 |
| 40 | 0.022 | 0.015 | 0.011 | 0.008 | 0.005 | 0.004 | 0.003 | 0.002 | 0.001 |
| 50 | 0.009 | 0.005 | 0.003 | 0.002 | 0.001 | 0.001 | 0.001 | 0.001 | |

# Appendix 1

## Glossary of Terms

To identify the meaning of all accountancy jargon is an almost impossible task, particularly since all organisations also tend to develop some special terms of their own! However, the following glossary will hopefully identify the main terms we are likely to meet:

**Accrual**
An estimated or provisional amount for an invoice not yet received.

**Added Value**
Total sales revenue less the cost of bought in materials and services.

**Asset**
Something of value owned by the business which has a measurable cost.

## Balance Sheet
A report showing the assets owned by a company and the way they have been financed. A snapshot of the position at a given moment in time.

## Calendarisation
Analysing annual budget totals into appropriate monthly amounts.

## Capital Expenditure
Money spent on Fixed Assets

## Cash Flow
The difference between cash receipts and cash payments during a certain period.

## Cash Flow Statement
A document showing movements on working capital, expenditure on fixed assets, sources of funds, (shares, loans) etc. in relation to profit achieved.

## Creditor
One who lends money or gives credit - typically suppliers.

## Current assets
Assets which are used in the operation of the business. Things which will constantly change with usage. Stock, debtors, cash.

## Debtors
One who owes us money – the unpaid invoices of customers.

## Debtor Days
A calculation of the number of days of sales on which payment is outstanding. A measure of the length of credit being allowed to Debtors.

## Deferred Taxation
Corporation tax deferred by Capital Allowances as substituted by the Inland Revenue exceeding provision for deprecation in the calculation of profits.

## Depreciation
That part of the value of a fixed asset which is written off because of a reduction in its working life – the proportion of the value "used up" during a given period.

## Direct Cost
A cost directly attributed to a product, service or production unit. Likely to be volume related.

## Discounted Cash flow
Techniques for discounting future returns from investments into today's cash value in order to compare alternative courses of capital investment activity or project spending. Includes both Net Present Value and Internal Rate of Return methods.

## Dividends
The amount of a business's profits that are distributed to shareholders.

## Earnings per share
Profit after tax, divided by the number of ordinary shares.

## Forecast
Estimated expenditure & variances to budget for the remaining months of the financial year.

## Fixed Asset
Assets retained for long-term use in the business e.g. property, equipment etc.

## Fixed Cost
A cost which does not vary automatically with changes in the volume of activity.

## Flexible Budget
A budget which can be flexed for different levels of activity according to unit costs involved.

## Gearing
Ratio of loan capital to share capital. The higher the gearing the larger the percentage of loan capital and the greater the need to pay interest regardless of the level of profit achieved.

## Goodwill
An intangible asset to a business that can appear on the balance sheet. A business is not only "worth" the total value of its fixed and current assets. Good management, a useful location, a reputation built up over the years etc., add to its "worth" which will have had to be paid for if the business has been acquired (goodwill is the excess of the purchase price over the book value of net assets acquired).

## Gross Profit
Total revenue/sales less cost of goods sold.

## Income
If used in the Profit and loss Account, an alternative term for turnover or sales.

## Income & Expenditure Account
Used in place of a Profit & Loss Account for non-profit making organisations, revealing any surplus or deficit on its activities. Charities are likely to replace this with a "Statement of Financial Activities" in the near future, which

will be more a mixture of the Income & Expenditure Account and a Cash Flow Statement in order to reveal movements in funding and debts used to support their charitable purposes.

**Indirect Expenses, Administration Expenses, Selling and Distribution Expenses**
Other costs which cannot be allocated distinctly to the products sold. Will include fixed costs as well as semi variable costs.

**Investment**
Amount invested in a major asset or in another company.

**Liabilities**
Amounts to be paid to others. The claims of outsiders against the assets of the business.

**Limiting Factor**
That which controls levels of activity for all budgets e.g. available capacity, level of sales etc.

**Liquidity**
Availability of cash or assets easily turned into cash to meet current obligations i.e. debtors and cash. A business is clearly liquid (or solvent) if a high proportion of assets are liquid.

**Net**
1 Figure after deduction
2 Payment of the full amount with no allowance for cash discount.

**Net Assets**
Total Assets less current liabilities (or Fixed Assets plus Working Capital). see also Return on Net Assets.

**Net Current Assets**
Working Capital. The difference of Current Assets less Current Liabilities.

**Net Interest**
Any interest payable to lenders of money, such as banks and debenture holders, less any interest from the company's own bank or investments.

**Operating Expenses**
An indirect cost or expense not attributed to a product.

**Operating Profit**
Gross profit less operating expenses, selling and distribution costs, depreciation, etc.

**Payables**
Alternative name for creditors.

**Plant**
Equipment and machinery.

**Profiling**
Alternative name for creditors.

**Profit**
Net income, excess of revenue over costs and expenses.

**Profit before Tax**
Operating profit less net interest and non-operating expenses.

**Profit and loss Account (P & L)**
Income statement showing sales, costs, expenses and resulting profit.

## Provision (e.g. for bad debts)

A cost based on a reasonable assessment of something which cannot be identified with absolute certainty e.g. it may be reasonable to suppose that say, 2½% of the amount owed to us by debtors at year end will not be paid – even though we can't identify the actual bad debts at this stage. Any subsequent difference between actual and provision will be carried forward to the next year.

## Receivables

Alternative name for Debtors.

## Retained Profit or Transferred to Reserves

Profits not paid to shareholders, retained in the business to finance future growth. Retained profit represents the amount the company has grown by its activities.

## Return on Capital Employed

See Return on Net Assets below (although definitions of the calculation vary).

## Return on Net assets

A measure of profit as a percentage of the funds tied up in the assets of the business. Net Assets may therefore be regarded as Total Assets less Current Liabilities, since to deduct long-term liabilities from the calculation would be to imply that the return on the funding they provide is not important.

## Revenue

Alternative name for Sales or Turnover in the Profit and Loss Account.

## Revenue Budget

One which deals with costs chargeable against revenue or income in the P & L account – as distinct from Capital

Budget items (for which only depreciation will be charged to the P & L)

**Share Capital**
Money put into the business by the owners.

**Shareholders**
Owners of shares in the company.

**Tax**
Corporation Tax payable on profits by a company.

**Turnover**
The value of sales achieved. It includes both cash and credit sales but not the sale of fixed assets or VAT.

**Variable Cost**
That part of a cost which varies with changes in the volume of business activity. A tighter definition than direct costs.

**Variance**
Difference between actual & budgeted cost (or income).

**Virement**
Procedure by which budget provisions can be approved for transfer from one expenditure category or cost centre to another.

**Working Capital**
Stocks, debtors and cash: Less current liabilities.

**Zero-based Budget**
One which has to be justified from scratch as if it were an entirely new business proposition. Used as a discipline to encourage more radical and cost efficient ways of running the organization.

# Appendix 2

## The Budgeting Process: Seven Steps to Success (summary)

1 Define Objectives
within the context of the longer term corporate plan

2 Define responsibility
the boundaries of your control, all the resources for which you are accountable and any changes.

3 Gather the facts
establish sources of information and policy guidelines (e.g. activity levels, inflation assumptions) for the up-coming budget round. Start collecting the records required well before your planned time for "number crunching".

## 4 Decide what to submit

and keep a record of what facts/estimates your decisions were based on. Gather ideas from your staff where you can.

## 5 Test and check

do the overall totals stack up? What about the monthly 'profiling' of individual income or expenditure lines? Are there other ways of meeting our objectives and responsibilities?

## 6 Win Approval

use the back-up detail to explain your submission to your boss and to the finance function. Recognise the need for adjustment to be consistent with other budgets to achieve the right overall plan.

## 7 Live with the budget

monitor and explain significant variances. Beware of "time lags" in charges appearing on statements. Prepare rolling forecasts (use as pointers for next year's budget also).